SAMUEL WILSON

1766 - 1854

WHO WAS "UNCLE SAM"

ILLUSTRATED STORY
OF THE LIFE OF OUR NATIONAL SYMBOL

by Cecile and Jean-Pierre Mouraux

*This book is dedicated
to Samuel Wilson
and the first generation
of Americans who built
the strong foundation
of our country.*

© 2006 Cecile and Jean-Pierre Mouraux
UNCLE SAM MUSEUM
Frame and cover designed by Basile Fattal
Published by Poster Collector
Printed In the United States
ISBN: 978-0-9786354-0-4
0-9786354-0-X

SAMUEL WILSON
"UNCLE SAM"

🎩 INTRODUCTION 🎩

An old French proverb says that *"You don't know a river if you don't know its source"*. This can't better characterize our national symbol. Everybody knows Uncle Sam, but few know his origins and the man behind the symbol.

WHO WAS UNCLE SAM?

We asked this question hundreds of times.
Generally, the answers are as follows:
- A fictitious character
- My boss: I work for the government
- The I.R.S.
- "I Want You", the famous WWI poster
- A meat-packer...

Very few know who was the real Uncle Sam, his story, and his role in the beginning of the United States.

The goal of this book is to help you discover the outstanding life of the man whose nickname became our national symbol. This is the story of the life of Samuel Wilson, through the beginning of the Revolution, various facts and anecdotes which made history, and the artists who made Uncle Sam famous.

SAMUEL WILSON
"UNCLE SAM"

ABOUT THE AUTHORS

Jean-Pierre and Cecile Mouraux flank a portrait
they commissioned of "Uncle Sam" Wilson,
whose Mason home they now own. (GIL BLISS)

Cecile and Jean-Pierre Mouraux own an original vintage poster business and they are significant poster collectors in their own right.

They compiled several important "theme" collections:
250 "Cats and Dogs" posters, 350 "International Red Cross" posters, 800 "WWI" posters, and 800 "Uncle Sam" posters and prints. They have also assisted clients in developing their personal collections.

"For us, a poster is not just a piece of paper. It is the story of a theme, historical or commercial, of an era, of an artist. Deep research enabled us to make some fascinating discoveries", they say.

One day, they acquired a WWI poster depicting "Uncle Sam" and they decided to know more about the character. *"It was a turn in our lives."*

The research lead them to find out who this famous unknown person was, to open an "Uncle Sam" Museum, to buy the Uncle Sam Wilson's family farm and to become an Uncle Sam historian.

"More than a hobby, it's our mission to help people learn who Samuel Wilson, this outstanding individual who became our nation's symbol, Uncle Sam, was."

They decided to entice you to share their passion.
That's the goal of this book.

SAMUEL WILSON
"UNCLE SAM"

CONTENTS

Dedication
Introduction.. 1
About the Authors.. 2
Recognition of Samuel Wilson as the official Uncle Sam.................. 4
Samuel Wilson's Trail.. 5
Wilson's Family History.. 6
Boston Massacre.. 10
Boston Tea Party.. 16
Samuel Wilson "Messenger of the Revolution".................................. 18
Paul Revere's Ride.. 19
Concord-Lexington-Menotomy Battle.. 24
Battle of Bunker Hill.. 30
The Wilson Family in Mason, New Hampshire................................... 36
The Mann House.. 48
Captain Benjamin Mann... 50
Johnny Appleseed.. 53
Samuel Wilson in Troy, New York... 54
Samuel Wilson "Brickmaker".. 56
Samuel Wilson "Meat-Packer".. 58
Samuel Wilson becomes America's Uncle Sam.................................. 59
Jonas W. Gleason... 62
Samuel Wilson's House in Troy.. 63
Samuel Wilson in Catskill, New York.. 64
Oakwood Cemetery in Troy... 65
Uncle Sam's Monument in Troy.. 66
Samuel Wilson as "Uncle Sam".. 67
Samuel Wilson and the Church... 68
Samuel Wilson and Politics.. 70
Samuel Wilson and the Community.. 71
From Samuel Wilson/Uncle Sam to Uncle Sam/U.S. Government.. 74
Samuel Wilson's Four Towns.. 80
Conclusion... 90
Acknowledgments... 91
Comments.. 92
Bibliography.. 94

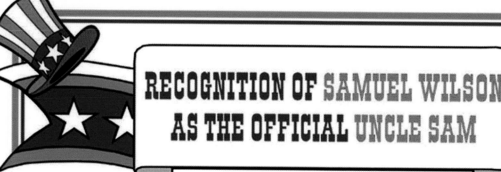

RECOGNITION OF SAMUEL WILSON AS THE OFFICIAL UNCLE SAM

 On September 15, 1961, the 87th Congress of the United States passed a joint resolution: The bill saluted the *"strength and idealism that characterized the life of Samuel Wilson"* and recognized Samuel Wilson of Troy, New York, as the progenitor of America's national symbol *Uncle Sam.* The bill was signed by President John Fitzgerald Kennedy.

 Proclamation of the Commonwealth of Massachusetts, by his Excellency John A. Volpe in 1966:

Whereas Samuel Wilson, born in Arlington, Massachusetts, on September 13, 1766, has given us the name of "Uncle Sam" which is recognized throughout the world as a symbol of the United States, and

Whereas, He contributed his services as a courier during the Revolutionary War and a provision supplier to the Army during the War of 1812, at which time his initials became synonymous with those of our country, and

Whereas, Uncle Sam has come to represent a combination of honesty, independence and justice, and leaves behind his name as a reminder to all Americans the citizenry of the freedom they enjoy, and of the responsibility they have to retain it;

Now, Therefore, I, JOHN A. VOLPE, Governor of the Commonwealth of Massachusetts, do hereby proclaim September 13, 1966, as

"UNCLE SAM DAY"

and urge all citizens of the Commonwealth to take full recognition of this day and pay tribute to a man who gave his name, as well as his time and energies to the United States.

Given. At the executive Chamber in Boston, this second day of September, in the year of our Lord, one thousand nine hundred and sixty-six, and to the Independence of the United States of America, the one hundred and ninety first.

JOHN A. VOLPE	*KEVIN P. WHITE*
His Excellency the Governor	Secretary of the Commonwealth

God Save the Commonwealth of Massachusetts

 In 1959, the New York legislature passed a resolution recognizing Samuel Wilson as Uncle Sam. His birthday, September 13th, was declared *Uncle Sam Day* by Governor Nelson Rockefeller.

 President Ronald Reagan designated September 13th as *Uncle Sam Day* across the nation. This resolution was passed on November 9, 1988, and became proclamation # 6016.

Samuel Wilson's Trail

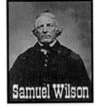

Samuel Wilson

Troy, NY
1789 - 1854

Mason, NH
1780 - 1789

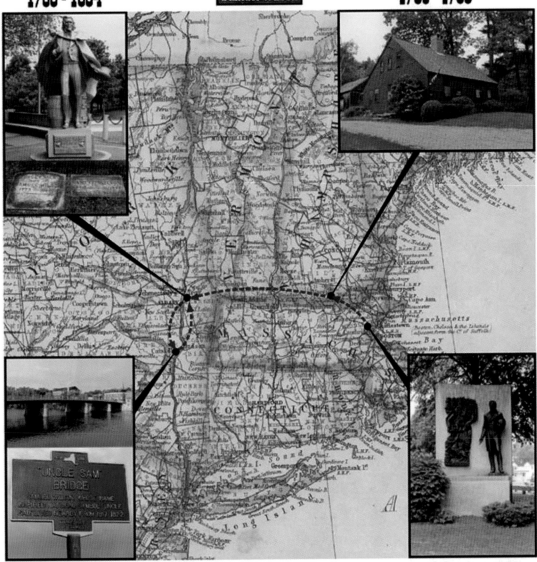

Catskill, NY
1817 - 1822

Arlington, MA
1766 - 1780

UNCLE SAM

SAMUEL WILSON
"UNCLE SAM"

WILSON'S FAMILY HISTORY

In the seventeenth century three "Wilson" brothers emigrated from Greenock, Scotland. They settled in the English American Colony: one in Connecticut, another one in New York, the third one, Robert Wilson, in Medford, Massachusetts. In 1665, Robert bought a farm in Menotomy, MA. Samuel Wilson is descended from this branch of the Wilsons.

Edward Wilson, Samuel's father, was born in 1734. In 1758, he married Lucy Francis who was born in Medford in 1739. Edward (1734-1816) and Lucy (1739-1835) made the Menotomy farm their home. Menotomy later became West Cambridge, then Arlington.

Edward and Lucy had thirteen children: Joseph (1759-?), Lucy (1761-1819), Edward (1762-1843), Ebenezer (1763-1825), Rachel (1765-1846), Samuel (1766-1854), Nathaniel (1768-1854), William (1769-?), Aaron (1771-?), a still-born baby (1772), Francis (1774-?), Andrew (1777-1841), and Thomas (1778-1862).

Samuel Wilson married Betsey Mann (1773-1863) on January 3, 1797. They had four children: Polly (1797-1805), Sam (1800-1807), Benjamin (1802-1859) and Albert (1805-1866). There may have been a fifth still-born child. Polly died from a fever when she was eight years old and Sam died at seven from a skull fracture after he fell from a wagon. Only Benjamin and Albert reached adulthood.

Benjamin became a lawyer. He practiced in Troy and in New York City. He passed away in 1859 from "Isthmus fever", which he contracted in Panama on his way to California. He married Mary Wood in Auburn, NY, in 1839. They had four children: Sarah born in Troy in 1841 died in 1845; Elizabeth died in her first year; Emma born in New York City in 1844 never married and died in 1916; and Marion born in 1849. Marion married Frederick Sheldon in Fairbault, MN, in 1876, and they had two sons, Carlton Wood Sheldon, born in 1880; and Harry born in 1882 died the same year. Carlton married Lily Porkers and they had a daughter Helen Marion who married Robert Brockett. They in turn had a daughter, Betty Sheldon born in 1930. She married William Joseph Hambuchen from Convoy, AK. They had two children, Helen and Robert who are the last direct descendants of Samuel Wilson.

Albert (1805-1866), Samuel's youngest son, remained close to his parents in Troy. He became a silversmith and a banjo maker. It's said that he never married nor had children but, in a letter dated July 17, 1936, sent by Mrs. Clara Wilson Hick from Brooklyn, NY, to the editor of the Troy Record, she states that Albert married but never had children.

SAMUEL WILSON
"UNCLE SAM"

BIRTH OF SAMUEL WILSON
IN MENOTOMY
(NOW ARLINGTON, MA)
SEPTEMBER 13, 1766

The Wilson farm was located in
the center of a triangle limited by
Massachusetts Avenue,
Mystic Street and Russell Street,
where now stands the
Uncle Sam Memorial Statue

SAMUEL WILSON
"UNCLE SAM"

SAMUEL WILSON'S BIRTHDAY

On the photo of the church birth record, it looks as though Samuel Wilson's date of birth was September 14, 1766.

This uncovers a little discrepancy because in all the following documents we read the date was September 13, 1766:
- in the Commonwealth of Massachusetts proclamation in 1966
- in the State of New York resolution declaring September 13th "Uncle Sam Day"
- in the bill signed by Ronald Reagan on November 9, 1988, designating September 13th as Uncle Sam Day
- during the inaugural address of the Samuel Wilson monument in Arlington on September 11, 1976.

On the other hand, in the book "History of Mason" published in 1858, the date is September 16, 1766. That might just be a mistake.

According to James J. Golden, Town Clerk in 1958, it is recorded that Samuel Wilson was born on September 13, 1766, in Arlington, Massachusetts. (*Vital Records to 1850, published in 1904*).

It seems most likely that Samuel Wilson was born on September 13th and his birth was recorded at the church on the following day when he was baptized.

SAMUEL WILSON
"UNCLE SAM"

BIRTH RECORD

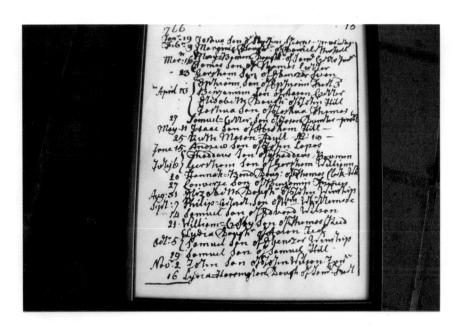

Samuel Wilson's birth record
from the Church archives

SAMUEL WILSON
"UNCLE SAM"

BOSTON MASSACRE
March 5, 1770

When Samuel was 4 years old, he attended the funerals of the victims of the Boston Massacre with his parents Edward and Lucy.

SAMUEL WILSON
"UNCLE SAM"

BOSTON MASSACRE

The Stamp Act, and later the Townshend Acts, which taxed the Bostonians, were at the origin of the colonist's displeasure. These taxes were imposed without vote or consultation of the people. Samuel Adams, the leader of the "Sons of Liberty", organized several demonstrations. One of them led to the Boston massacre.

During a cold night in March 1770, a group of sixty rowdy Bostonians assailed a small patrol of British soldiers with insults, snowballs, stones and garbage. One of the British soldiers slipped and fell down. The other ones, thinking that he had been wounded and fearing for their lives, opened fire. Five demonstrators were killed and six were hurt. Though it was not properly so called a "massacre", it inflamed the anger of the Bostonians. Three days later, over 10,000 people attended the funerals of the victims in Boston. Among them was the Wilson family from Menotomy.

The plate depicting the Boston massacre engraved by Paul Revere, a friend of Samuel Adams, was printed and sent to the rest of the colonies. It nurtured an anti-British spirit which only recessed with the Independence of the USA.

A cousin of Samuel Adams, John Adams, was a lawyer. He, with Josiah Quincy, defended successfully the head of the British soldiers, Captain Preston, and the regulars. He stated: "*On that night, the foundation of American Independence was laid*".

SAMUEL WILSON
"UNCLE SAM"

BOSTON MASSACRE

A circle of cobblestones marks the site of
the Boston massacre, in front of the
Old State House

SAMUEL WILSON
"UNCLE SAM"

BOSTON MASSACRE

CRANARY BURIAL GROUND
1660

WITHIN THIS GROUND ARE BURIED

THE VICTIMS OF THE BOSTON MASSACRE,

MARCH 5, 1770.

JOSIAH FRANKLIN AND WIFE,

(Parents of Benjamin Franklin)

PETER FANEUIL,   PAUL REVERE;

AND

JOHN PHILLIPS,

FIRST MAYOR OF BOSTON.

**FRONT GATE OF THE GRANARY BURIAL GROUND
BOSTON**

SAMUEL WILSON
"UNCLE SAM"

BOSTON MASSACRE

**VIEW OF THE GRANARY BURIAL GROUND
BOSTON, MASSACHUSETTS**

Named after the early colonial grain storage facility that once stood on the adjacent site of the Park Street Church, the cemetery dates from 1660.

Three important signatories to the Declaration of Independence (John Hancock, Samuel Adams and Robert Treat Paine) are buried here along with Benjamin Franklin's parents, the merchant Peter Faneuil, Paul Revere, Doctor Warren, John Phillips *first Mayor of Boston*, and the victims of the Boston Massacre.

SAMUEL WILSON
"UNCLE SAM"

BOSTON MASSACRE

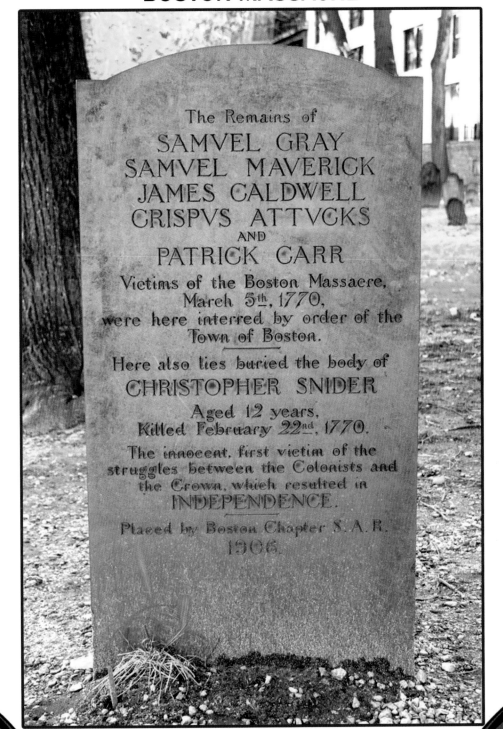

TOMB OF THE VICTIMS

SAMUEL WILSON
"UNCLE SAM"

BOSTON TEA PARTY

On December 16, 1773,
Edward Wilson, Samuel's father,
disguised as a Mohawk Indian,
participated in the Boston Tea Party.

SAMUEL WILSON
"UNCLE SAM"

BOSTON TEA PARTY
DECEMBER 16, 1773

The British East India Company had controlled all tea trading between India and the British Colonies. As a result of the tea tax, the Colonies refused to buy the British tea. Instead, they smuggled tea in from Holland. This left the British East India Company with warehouses full of unsold tea, and the company was in danger of going out of business.

To prevent that, in May 1773, the British Parliament passed the "Tea Act" which allowed the British East India Company to sell directly to the colonists, by-passing the colonial wholesale merchants.

The merchants, headed by Samuel Adams, organized the "Boston Tea Party". On the evening of December 16, 1773, three groups of men, calling themselves the *Sons of Liberty*, disguised as Mohawk Indians, boarded three English tea ships (the Beaver, the Eleanor and the Dartmouth) at Griffin's Wharf and dumped their freight of 342 chests of tea, which was valued at more than 10,000 pounds, into the waters of the Boston harbor.

In retaliation, King George III and the British Parliament responded by closing the city port and sent four British regiments to Boston along with a new Governor General, Thomas Gage.

SAMUEL WILSON
"UNCLE SAM"

SAMUEL WILSON
"MESSENGER OF THE REVOLUTION"

It was in early fall in 1774. Samuel, just eight years old, was an alert and intelligent boy. Immersed in the beginning of the Revolution and used to the hard labor of the farm, he already had the maturity of a young adult and was very responsible.

On his way to the parish of Reverend Cook one day, Samuel spotted a stranger riding his horse through the village, taking notes and drawing sketches. Samuel rushed to alert the Reverend Cook who also was the coordinator of the messengers of Dr. Joseph Warren for his area. He also concealed the arms and ammunition of the Patriots in his parish. Cook asked Samuel to watch the stranger who was certainly spying for the Tories. Upon hearing young Samuel's report of the stranger's activities, Cook decided to send a messenger to warn Dr. Warren. Samuel volunteered and convinced the reluctant Reverend Cook that a young boy would go unnoticed more easily than an adult. Reverend Cook accepted, provided that Samuel's father would give his approval.

Edward Wilson did agree and even made up an alibi for his son: some medicine to buy for his young brother Francis who was sick. He wrote the name of the medicine on a piece of paper which he gave to Samuel.

Samuel took the Cambridge Boston road. He was promptly caught up by the stranger who asked him where he was going. Samuel told his story. Suspicious, the stranger proposed to Samuel that he would escort him to the apothecary.

Once there, the stranger grabbed the paper from Samuel's hands to verify that it was not a message the young boy was carrying. Convinced by the note, the stranger left the shop. Samuel received his medicine and was told where to find Dr. Warren.

When Samuel exited the shop, he found the stranger waiting for him outside, who offered to accompany him back to Menotomy. After a few miles, finally assured that Samuel was not pretending, he turned back. Samuel kept on riding towards Menotomy for a while to make sure that the Tory was not following him, then turned back to join Dr. Warren and inform him of the presence of the spy in Menotomy. Dr. Warren congratulated Samuel and entrusted him with a another message this time for the Reverend Cook instructing him to move the arms and ammunition to another hiding-place. Impressed by the success of his first mission, Dr. Warren and the Reverend Cook decided to further retain the young Samuel as a messenger.

SAMUEL WILSON
"UNCLE SAM"

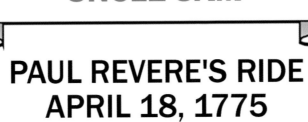

PAUL REVERE'S RIDE
APRIL 18, 1775

When Samuel Wilson was eight years old, he
witnessed the famous midnight ride of Paul Revere.
On his way from Boston to Lexington to warn
Samuel Adams and John Hancock that the English
were coming, Paul Revere crossed the Wilson's
property to alert Samuel's father,
Edward Wilson, a minuteman and a
"Son of Liberty".

SAMUEL WILSON
"UNCLE SAM"

RESIDENCE OF REV. JOHN HANCOCK IN LEXINGTON

JOHN HANCOCK

SAMUEL ADAMS

SAMUEL WILSON
"UNCLE SAM"

END OF PAUL REVERE'S RIDE
April 19, 1775

At 2:00 AM, at this point between Lexington and Concord, ended the midnight ride of Paul Revere.

After he completed his mission and awakened Samuel Adams and John Hancock in Lexington, Paul Revere rode to Concord to warn the Concord patriots. He was intercepted by the English, who brought him back to Lexington where he was released. That same morning he rejoined Adams and Hancock.

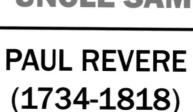

PAUL REVERE
(1734-1818)

Paul Revere was the son of a French immigrant artisan. He was gifted with numerous talents:

- He was a famous silversmith/craftsman.

- He was a plate engraver (he engraved the plate of the Boston Massacre).

- He also worked as a dentist (he not only cleaned teeth but also wired in false teeth carved from walrus ivory or other animal teeth).

- He was a political activist and a patriot (he was employed by the Boston Committe of Correspondence and the Massachusetts Committee of Safety as an express rider to carry news, messages, and copies of resolutions as far away as New York and Philadelphia).

- He served as lieutenant colonel in the Massachusetts State Train of Artillery and commander of Castle Island in Boston Harbor.

- He opened a foundry which supplied bolts, spikes, and nails for the North End ship-yards (including brass fittings for the *U.S.S. Constitution*). He produced canons and, after 1792, cast bells (one of his largest bells still rings in the Boston King's Chapel).

- He opened the first copper rolling mill in North America in 1801 (he provided copper sheeting for the hull of the U.S.S. Constitution and the dome of the new Massachusetts State House in 1803).

He died on May 10, 1818, at the age of 83 years.

SAMUEL WILSON
"UNCLE SAM"

PAUL REVERE

(1734-1818)

Paul Revere was buried at the
Granary Burial Ground
in Boston

SAMUEL WILSON
"UNCLE SAM"

CONCORD - LEXINGTON - MENOTOMY BATTLE

In April 1775, the British governor, General Gage, learned that the colonists had stored weapons and ammunition in Concord and that two most active rebel leaders, Samuel Adams and John Hancock, were hiding in Lexington. He sent troops to capture the two leaders and destroy the arms, hoping that the success of this action would definitively bring the ongoing trouble in Massachusetts to an end.

Dr. Joseph Warren, leader of the "Committee of Safety", sent two messengers, Paul Revere and William Dawes, to alert Adams and Hancock on one hand, and to warn the Concord patriots on the other hand. On his way to Lexington, Paul Revere woke up all the minutemen along the road.

The two messengers completed the first part of their mission, but were captured on their way to Concord. William Dawes managed to escape and reach Concord. Paul Revere was arrested and released the following morning.

Six hundred British troops, under Colonel Francis Smith and Major Pitcairn were sent from Boston to Lexington. A verbal clash between the British soldiers and the patriots turned violent and guns were fired leaving eight patriots dead and fourteen wounded. Another combat occurred across the Concord North bridge where two militia men and three British soldiers were killed. The British decided to return to Boston. On their way back, they were attacked by the minutemen, especially in Menotomy. The British officers found themselves unable to hold their enraged troops who invaded and burned houses and put their occupants to death. The British lost some 250 men in this first bloody battle of the Revolution.

SAMUEL WILSON
"UNCLE SAM"

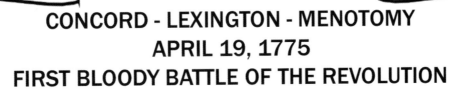

CONCORD - LEXINGTON - MENOTOMY
APRIL 19, 1775
FIRST BLOODY BATTLE OF THE REVOLUTION

Edward Wilson, Samuel's father, joined the minutemen in
Lexington. Samuel, in Menotomy, was the witness
to three important events:
❧ The first prisoners of war
❧ The fight of Samuel Whittemore
❧ And the killing of Jason Russell

SAMUEL WILSON
"UNCLE SAM"

THE FIRST PRISONERS
OF THE REVOLUTIONARY WAR

In front of what was then the Congregational Church, a tablet indicates:

AT THIS SPOT
ON APRIL 19,1775
THE OLD MEN OF MENOTOMY
CAPTURED A CONVOY OF
EICHTEEN SOLDIERS WITH SUPPLIES
ON ITS WAY TO JOIN
THE BRITISH AT LEXINGTON.

On April 19th, Samuel remained in Menotomy with his mother and young brothers and sisters while his father and his older brothers joined the other minutemen in Lexington. That day, Samuel witnessed the first of three significant events that occurred close to the Wilson's farm.

A convoy of two wagons with food and ammunition that followed the English army towards Lexington took a wrong turn and was separated from the main body.

Only a few older men unable to follow the patriots were staying in Menotomy. They were veterans of the French-Indian war and skilled in the handling of muskets. They ordered the soldiers to stop. As they refused to obey, the veterans shot their horses and killed two of the soldiers. Others fled through the fields until they encountered Mother Batherick, a huge old lady who was digging dandelions. The soldiers soon surrendered to the great lady.

Before she lead her six prisoners - the first ones of the Revolutionary war - to the house of Captain Ephraim Frost, Mother Batherick told them: *"If you survive and get back home, tell King George that an old woman captured six of his grenadiers."*

In England the incident was caught up scornfully by the opposition papers which asked: *"If one old yankee woman can take six grenadiers, how many soldiers will it require to conquer America?"*

SAMUEL WILSON
"UNCLE SAM"

CONCORD - LEXINGTON - MENOTOMY BATTLE

NEAR THIS SPOT

SAMUEL WHITTEMORE,

THEN 80 YEARS OLD,

KILLED THREE BRITISH SOLDIERS

APRIL 19, 1775.

HE WAS SHOT BAYONETED,

BEATEN AND LEFT FOR DEAD,

BUT RECOVERED AND LIVED

TO BE 98 YEARS OF AGE.

The fight between Samuel Whittemore
and the English soldiers occurred a
few yards from the Wilson's farm.

SAMUEL WILSON
"UNCLE SAM"

CONCORD - LEXINGTON - MENOTOMY BATTLE

The Jason Russell house where Jason Russell and 11 Patriots perished on April 19, 1775, is now the home of the Arlington (MA.) Historical Society and the Smith Museum.

SAMUEL WILSON
"UNCLE SAM"

CONCORD - LEXINGTON - MENOTOMY BATTLE

The victims of the Menotomy battle
(English soldiers and Patriots)
were buried in the old cemetery of Arlington, MA.

SAMUEL WILSON
"UNCLE SAM"

BATTLE OF BUNKER HILL
JUNE 17, 1775

Edward Wilson fought with the minutemen in the battle of Bunker Hill in Charlestown along with Captain Benjamin Mann, future father-in-law of Samuel. Captain Mann had come from Mason, New Hampshire, with 26 volunteers.

Samuel was sent to Boston as a messenger by the Committee of Safety to observe the battle from the heights of Beacon Hill and report the events to the people of Menotomy and Cambridge.

SAMUEL WILSON
"UNCLE SAM"

BATTLE OF BUNKER HILL
JUNE 17, 1775

Samuel's father was wounded at the battle of Bunker Hill and Joseph Warren, the doctor who recruited Samuel as a messenger, was killed.

The English counted 1,100 casualties, and the Patriots 400.

That was the last battle conducted by the minutemen. Two weeks later, on July 2, 1775, General George Washington went to Cambridge and created the New Continental Army. He assumed the role of Commander-in-Chief.

SAMUEL WILSON
"UNCLE SAM"

BUNKER HILL MONUMENT

Monument erected in memory of the Battle of Bunker Hill. In 1825, the Marquis de Lafayette, hero of the American Revolution, laid the cornerstone of the monument.

SAMUEL WILSON
"UNCLE SAM"

BUNKER HILL MONUMENT

Dr. JOSEPH WARREN
1741-1775

Dr. Joseph Warren created and headed the Provincial Committee of Safety (intelligence service of the Patriots). A few days before the battle he was commissioned second major general. He postponed his acceptance of this position to fight at the battle of Bunker Hill as a volunteer minuteman. He fell heroically in the battle and was buried at the Old Granary cemetery.

SAMUEL WILSON
"UNCLE SAM"

COLONEL WILLIAM PRESCOTT
1726-1795

William Prescott was born in Groton, MA. in 1726 and later settled in Pepperell, MA.

In 1755, he served successfully as lieutenant and captain during the British expedition against Nova Scotia. He declined a commission in the regular army and he retired to his estate in Pepperell.

In 1774, he was appointed to command a regiment of minutemen. In 1775, he went to Lexington with his regiment to oppose the expedition that was sent out by General Thomas Gage.

On June 16, 1775, he was ordered to Charlestown with 1,200 men and the day after he participated in the battle of Bunker Hill. Bancroft said that "his bravery could never be acknowledged and applauded enough". He was one of the last to leave the entrenchments.

In 1777, he resigned from the continental army and returned to Pepperell. The same year, he rejoined the northern army under General Horatio Gates as a volunteer and took part in the battle of Saratoga.

He died in Pepperell on October 13, 1795.

SAMUEL WILSON
"UNCLE SAM"

BUNKER HILL MONUMENT

Statue of Colonel William Prescott who, as head of 1,200
Massachusetts and Connecticut Patriots, fortified Breed's Hill.
Colonel Prescott is credited with the order
"Don't fire until you see the whites of their eyes".

SAMUEL WILSON
"UNCLE SAM"

1780
THE WILSON FAMILY
IN MASON, NEW HAMPSHIRE

The Wilson farm in Mason, NH

In 1780, Edward Wilson sold his farm in Menotomy, MA, to Thomas Russell, the store-keeper. He also sold the Medford farm his wife had inherited. He bought a farm on a 100-acre property in Mason, NH. He acquired a pair of oxen to help move their belongings and in April of that year, the Wilson family minus the two older sons, who had joined the Continental Army of General Washington in Valley Forge, proceeded to Mason.

HISTORICAL
UNCLE SAM HOUSE
MASON, NEW HAMPSHIRE

Mason, NH, is located close to the Massachusetts border.

The title to the township of Mason was granted on November 1, 1749. The town was incorporated in 1768 and, on June 28, 1872, Greenville (formerly Mason Village) separated from Mason and was incorporated as a separate town.

The New Hampshire Historical Society posted a sign in front of the Uncle Sam house. The historical Uncle Sam house is located at 187 Valley Road in Mason. Today it is owned by Cecile and Jean-Pierre Mouraux proprietors of the Uncle Sam Museum.

SAMUEL WILSON
"UNCLE SAM"

HISTORY OF THE
WILSON PROPERTY IN MASON, NH

The title to the township of Mason was granted on November 1, 1749, by an instrument of that date executed by Colonel Joseph Blanchard on behalf of the Masonian proprietors.

Colonel Joseph Blanchard, born in 1705 in Dunstable, NH, was a distinguished land surveyor. He prepared the first map of New Hampshire.

In his first grant, lot number 6, which was later owned by Edward Wilson, was drawn by Eleazer Blanchard, son of Joseph Blanchard.

Being not of legal age, he was excused from the duty of improving and settling the property until 1755 when he would be 24. Unfortunately, he departed this life on March 19, 1753, in the 22nd year of his life.

The next owner whose name is known, is Samuel Abbott who settled in Mason in 1772. He sold one acre of his property to the town for a burying place: "Pleasant View cemetery".

The actual farm was built in 1773. Samuel Abbott remained the owner of the property until 1780.

In April 1780, Edward Wilson arranged a purchase from Samuel Abbott for the sum of two thousand two hundred pounds lawful money of the lot number 6 in the 8th range in the township of Mason.

In 1840, close to the Wilson farm, an additional large house was built by Brooks Wilson, nephew of Samuel Wilson.

The Wilson house remained in the Wilson Family and its succeeding generations for 122 years, until the death of the last Wilson owner in 1902; Mrs. Persis J. Wilson was the widow of Thomas K. Wilson, who was the son of Captain Thomas A. Wilson, brother of Uncle Sam.

SAMUEL WILSON
"UNCLE SAM"

HISTORY OF THE
WILSON PROPERTY IN MASON, NH

HISTORY OF MASON.

RECORD OF THE DRAFT OF LOTS IN TOWNSHIP NO. 1.

NAMES.	Draught.	Number.	Range.	Number.	Range.	Number.	Range.	NAMES.	Draught.	Number.	Range.	Number.	Range.	Number.	Range.
Ministry,	1	5	7	3	5	1	17	John Stevens, Esq.,	35	8	11	9	9	3	3
School,	2	6	5	6	10	7	1	Samuel Moore and *	36	10	18	10	19	4	13
George Jaffrey,	3	10	1	9	8	8	4	Joseph Farrar †	37	2	15	8	5		
Peter Powers, *	4	9	1	2	6	1	5	Minister,	38	5	10	5	11	1	3
Eleazer Blanchard,	5	8	1	7	8	6	8	Joseph Blanchard, Jr.,	39	4	9	2	16	1	16
John Goff, Esq.,	6	5	8	4	4	2	2	Peter Powers, ‡	40	4	10	1	12	1	13
David Adams,†	7	9	2	4	5	3	6	J. P. §	41	4	12	1	11	1	7
Paul March,	8	10	2	4	7	5	1	Elnathan Blood,	42	3	12	3	11	3	19
Phillip Olerike,	9	9	3	6	6	2	5	Thomas Parker, Esq.,	43	8	13	1	10	2	10
Eleazer Farwell,	10	5	3	2	1	1	15	Mr. Thomas Packer,	44	6	13	1	19	3	18
John Stevens, Esq.,	11	4	3	5	4	4	2	J. P. ‖	45	3	13	2	18	7	12
Thomas Wallingford,	12	10	4	10	3	5	2	John Tufton Mason, Esq.,	46	7	20	7	13	2	13
Nathaniel Meserve, Jr.,	13	9	5	9	4	6	18	George March,	47	8	14	3	7	2	17
Peter Powers, Jr.,	14	5	5	5	6	1	6	Mark H. Wentworth,	48	6	14	5	14	2	7
Joseph Blodgett,	15	7	3	4	6	6	11	Capt. Robert Fletcher,	49	3	14	3	15	10	20
John Butterfield, ‡	16	7	6	4	1	0	0	Saml. Scollay and March,	50	5	13	6	20	1	14
Jonathan Powers, Jr.,	17	8	20	1	8	8	6	John Moffat, Esq.,	51	5	15	8	19	3	9
Mark Hunking Wentworth,	18	6	1	9	6	1	9	Jonathan Lawrence, [bard,	52	6	16	4	20	2	8
Thomas Taylor, §	19	16	6	10	5	4	8	Mr. Trowbridge, now Hub-	53	5	16	3	20	8	16
Matthew Livermore,	20	10	7	9	7	1	2	Amasa Parker.	54	4	16	1	20	5	12
John Stevens, Esq.,	21	10	14	7	9	5	9	Jona. Hubbard, Jr.,	55	3	16	3	17	7	14
William Lawrence, Esq.,	22	5	19	6	2	2	3	Jacob Gould,	56	4	14	4	18	2	12
William Parker, Esq.,	23	8	9	8	2	2	4	Wm. Lawrence, Esq.,	57	5	17	8	17	7	17
John Wentworth, Jr.,	24	8	8	7	7	2	9	Benja. Parker,	58	6	17	2	20	7	15
Maj. Jona. Hubbard,	25	10	9	10	8	3	4	Maj. Jona. Hubbard, J.P., ¶	59	9	17	9	16	6	12
Maj. Wm. Lawrence, ‖	26	7	10	7	11			Mr. David Stearns,	60	9	18	2	19	8	15
John Varnum, ¶	27	8	10	1	1	5	4	Capt Thomas Tarbell,	61	8	18	4	19	4	11
John Stevens, Esq.,	28	9	10	9	11	2	11	Joseph Blanchard, Esq.,	62	7	18	6	7	2	14
Josiah Brown,	29	10	10	8	3	8	7	Theodore Atkinson, Esq.,	63	5	18	5	20	3	8
Richard Wibird, Esq.,	30	7	4	7	2	1	4	Wm. Lawrence. Esq.,	64	6	3	6	4	4	17
Jotham Odiorn,	31	10	17	10	12	10	16	Capt. Saml. Tarbell,	65	7	19	6	19	4	15
Nathl. Meserve, Esq.,	32	10	15	9	12	9	15	Joshua Pierce,	66	9	19	9	20	6	15
John Gennison,	33	10	11	8	12	6	9	Shadrack Whitney,	67	3	1				
John Stevens, Esq.,	34	9	13	9	14	3	2								

The foregoing is a True Copy of the Draught and numbers of the lots In the Township No. One, so called, lying in the Province of New Hampshire, as they was Drawn by the Proprietors of said Township. A true copy. Examined and Recorded,

Pr JOHN STEVENS, Prop's Clerk.

First draft of lots in Mason, NH
1749

SAMUEL WILSON
"UNCLE SAM"

HISTORY OF THE WILSON PROPERTY IN MASON, NH "ANECDOTES"

* Samuel Abbott, who owned the property from 1772 until 1780, enlisted in Mason with Captain Benjamin Mann's company along with 26 other volunteers who left for Cambridge on June 16, 1775, to join Colonel Reed's regiment of the future Continental Army for the battle of Bunker Hill. Edward Wilson, who bought the property, also engaged in the battle of Bunker Hill where he was wounded.

* One of the Boston Tea Party participants lived on the Wilson's orchard for about a year. The night of December 16, 1773, at Griffin's Wharf in Boston, Joshua Wyeth, age fifteen, a journeyman blacksmith, was among those disguised as Indians. Seven years later, he came to Mason and stayed a year or more in the Wilson's orchard. The "Indians" were sworn to secrecy but in 1827, when Joshua Wyeth was an old man, far away in Ohio, he told his story.

> Most of the persons selected for the occasion were apprentices and journeymen, not a few of them, as was the case with myself, living with tory masters. . . . Our numbers were between 28 and 30. . . . We first talked of firing the ships; but we feared the fire would communicate to the town. We then proposed sinking them; but we dropped this project. We finally concluded that we could take possession of them and discharge the tea into the harbor. To prevent being recognized, we agreed to wear ragged clothes and disfigure ourselves as much as possible; our faces were smeared with soot or lamp-black, and we should not have known each other except for our voices. We surely resembled devils from the bottomless pit rather than men.
>
> — from *The Boston Teaparty*, as told by Joshua Wyeth in 1827 to Rev. Timothy Flint

SAMUEL WILSON
"UNCLE SAM"

UNCLE SAM HOUSE
THROUGH THE YEARS

Barn and shed Circa 1900

House and barn Circa 1980

SAMUEL WILSON
"UNCLE SAM"

UNCLE SAM HOUSE
THROUGH THE YEARS

2005

SAMUEL WILSON
"UNCLE SAM"

UNCLE SAM HOUSE
MAIN ROOM

Top: date unknown   Bottom: 2005

UNCLE SAM HOUSE
"BORNING ROOM"

In 2004, in her article "History changing hands" for the Grapevine publication, Kathleen Baglio Humphreys writes:

"During a tour of the house, John and Penny Savard proudly showed off the king's board, which is any board over 14 inches, which should have been sent to England but somehow these pieces stayed in Mason. The dining room is very impressive with its "grain painted" wood. Grain painting occurred in the Victorian era when homeowners could not afford to use oak so the look of oak was simulated with a paintbrush. It is possible the wood in this room could be the largest collection of grain painting in the U.S. according to the N.Y. Museum of Folk Art.

"The house boasts a beautiful cooking fireplace in the dining room and wide pine floor boards. There is a "borning room", which was a little room with a little Ben Franklin fireplace. Exposed beams and horsehair plaster grace the ceilings. In the upstairs bathroom the brick chimney is exposed in a charming appeal."

SAMUEL WILSON
"UNCLE SAM"

THE WILSON PROPERTY
THE CASCADES

A stream, enhanced by a few waterfalls, runs through the Wilson property

These cascades were one of the Wilson children's favorite places to play. Samuel also took the cattle there to drink.

SAMUEL WILSON
"UNCLE SAM"

MASON, NH
PLEASANT VIEW CEMETERY

Mrs. Lucy Wilson

Captain Thomas Wilson

Miss Lucy Wilson

The Pleasant View cemetery was part of the Wilson property until 1772. There rest Mrs. Lucy Wilson, Samuel's mother, his sister Lucy, his brother Thomas, and numerous members of his extended family.

SAMUEL WILSON
"UNCLE SAM"

SAMUEL WILSON IN MASON
1780 - 1789

THE MANN HOUSE FIREPLACE

In Mason, as a teenager and a young adult, Samuel Wilson worked with his father on their farm where he learned to tend cattle and preserve meat.

In Brookline, a town close to Mason, he learned how to make bricks in a clay quarry.

Wishing to marry Betsey Mann and wanting to offer her a decent life, Samuel left Mason in February 1789 with his brother Ebenezer to make his fortune in Troy, New York. It took them 15 walking days in a cold winter to reach the village of Troy. He had asked Betsey to wait for his return and she promised to wait for him.

In 1797, eight years after his departure from Mason to Troy where he built his fortune with his brick factory and his meat-packing enterprise, Samuel came back to Mason to marry Betsey as promised. The wedding ceremony took place in the house of Captain Mann and the benediction was given by his childhood friend, the Reverend Ebenezer Hill, in front of the fireplace of the Mann house. Ebenezer Hill was nicknamed "the Little Minister of Mason" (five foot tall).

After the ceremony, Samuel and Betsey left for Troy.

SAMUEL WILSON
"UNCLE SAM"

THE MANN HOUSE
MASON, NEW HAMPSHIRE

The Mann store   The Mann house

This fine old colonial house is one of the few authentically certified old houses of historical note in New England. It was built in or about the year 1774, by Captain Benjamin Mann who appears to have been the leader in this community in those times, and who stood for the best of everything, "the public virtues of good government, good schools, good morals and sober industry".

In 1777, the public store of town powder was brought to Captain Mann's house and was kept in the present chimney vault in the cellar "for safekeeping and proper distribution".

At the same time Mann was given the right "to keep a tavern and a small store of goods". This was one of the first such taverns in New England.

SAMUEL WILSON
"UNCLE SAM"

THE MANN HOUSE
AND THE MANN STORE

The Mann house and the Mann store are located within walking distance from the Wilson farm. Samuel paid frequent visits to the Mann house and store. The main purpose of his visits was Betsey Mann, Captain Mann's daughter.

SAMUEL WILSON
"UNCLE SAM"

CAPTAIN BENJAMIN MANN
(1740-1831)
SAMUEL WILSON'S FATHER-IN-LAW

Circa 1771, Captain Benjamin Mann moved with his family from Woburn to Mason.

Soon after he came to Mason, he was employed in public offices in town:
- Moderator of the annual Mason town meeting for 12 years
- Town clerk for 4 years
- Selectman for 6 years.

He was also representative to the State legislature, a delegate to conventions, and a member of *the Committee of the Safety* and other important committees related to the Revolutionary War.

Benjamin Mann was the first person appointed Justice of the Peace in Mason.

SAMUEL WILSON
"UNCLE SAM"

CAPTAIN BENJAMIN MANN
(1740-1831)
SAMUEL WILSON'S FATHER-IN-LAW

The Captain's military record was impressive. He commanded a company in the army of Rhode Island and a company in the battle of Bunker Hill.

In 1774, Mann led in the voting "to suspend all commercial intercourse with the Island of Great Britain", and stated "we will not purchase nor use any wares or merchandise from Great Britain, except necessities, and will break off trade with any who do". This seems to be the first declaration of boycott in America.
Many discussions took place in the old Mann house in front of one of the six big old-fashioned fireplaces.

Following the commercial success of Samuel Wilson in Troy, NY, the Mann family moved there, where the E. S. Wilson Company employed many of them.

A Troy record shows a partnership between Samuel and his brother-in-law James Mann called Wilson & Mann. It was selling groceries and dry goods.

Benjamin Mann died in Troy in 1831 at the age of 91 years.
He was buried in the old Troy cemetery.

SAMUEL WILSON
"UNCLE SAM"

CAPTAIN BENJAMIN MANN
(1740-1831)
SAMUEL WILSON'S FATHER-IN-LAW

Anecdote

By 1815, a New Hampshire community had grown so much that it sought its own incorporation and looked for a name.

Captain Benjamin Mann suggested to the governor, John Taylor Gilman, who was his friend, the name of "Troy" as his daughter Betsey, Samuel Wilson's wife, lived in Troy, NY.

The proposition was accepted and a new town was born:
Troy, New Hampshire.

Monument dedicated to Captain Benjamin Mann
by the Mason Historical Society

SAMUEL WILSON
"UNCLE SAM"

JOHNNY APPLESEED

Johnny Appleseed was born on September 26, 1774, in Leominster, MA.
He died in 1845 in Indiana.

At the Mann house, young Samuel Wilson often met another young man, John Chapman, a cousin of Captain Mann, who visited his family in Mason.

It was said that he mostly came to see his cousin, Betsey Mann, with whom he had fallen in love.

He was the unlucky competitor of Samuel Wilson for Betsey's heart.

He later became Samuel's cousin when Samuel married Betsey.

John Chapman ultimately became another American legend under the nickname of *Johnny Appleseed*.

COINCIDENCE OR NOT?

In 1797, following Betsey and Samuel's wedding and their departure for Troy, NY, John Chapman stopped paying visits to Mason and started his hermit-pioneer life. He never married.

Did his romantic disappointment lead him to this new life style?
The facts and the dates would confirm this hypothesis.

SAMUEL WILSON
"UNCLE SAM"

TROY, NY
1789 - 1854

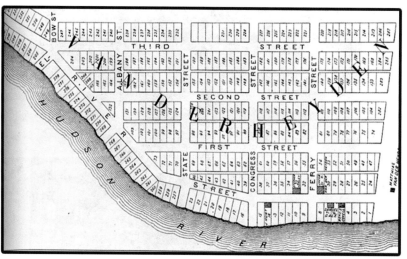

Circa 1789

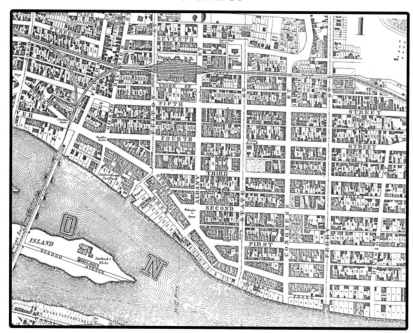

Circa 1854

Samuel Wilson and his brother Ebenezer arrived in Troy after 15 days on foot. Having walked their breadth of New Hampshire and Vermont, they reached a village in New York whose name had just been changed from Vanderheyden to Troy one month earlier. Samuel and Ebenezer took an active part in the expansion of the city.

SAMUEL WILSON
"UNCLE SAM"

SAMUEL WILSON
IN TROY

Wilson was one of the pioneers who turned the little village of Troy into a flourishing city.

He was an entrepreneur. He was engaged in, and successfully managed, at least five distinct kinds of businesses, continuously employing about 200 people while he took the oversight of each particular enterprise.

Along with his brother Ebenezer he operated:
* The mercantile business in connection with the slooping,
* The brick-making business on a large scale,
* The distillery business,
* Extensive farming,
* And the prosperous slaughtering business.

Wilson's management style was unique: For example, to his laborers, he would always say: "*Come boys*" instead of "*Go*". This approach enabled him to secure a greater amount of labor than other men.

SAMUEL WILSON
"UNCLE SAM"

SAMUEL WILSON
"BRICKMAKER"

Samuel and Ebenezer had brickmaking in their blood: their mother's grandfather, John Francis, a brickmaker, had helped build Harvard College, and two of their uncles were also brickmakers in Medford, Massachusetts.

In Mason, Sam and Ebenezer learned how to make bricks. However, there was no commercial outlet for this activity there.

Upon their arrival in Troy, they created the E. S. Wilson company which supplied fine bricks made from clay from the slopes of Mount Ida for homes and public buildings.

The first edifice to use these bricks was built by James Spencer in 1792 at the North-West corner of Second and Albany Streets. The Wilsons also furnished bricks for the first courthouse and jail of Rensselaer County in 1793.

The first Courthouse and Jail of Rensselaer County

SAMUEL WILSON
"UNCLE SAM"

SAMUEL WILSON
"BRICKMAKER"

These bricks come from one of the old Ferry Street warehouses that were built during Samuel Wilson's era and are now completely destroyed. They were most likely manufactured by the E. S. Wilson Company, the only brick factory at the time.

SAMUEL WILSON
"UNCLE SAM"

SAMUEL WILSON
"MEAT-PACKER"

The two brothers started their meat-packing business in 1793, in a meadow located where the Poestenkill enters the Hudson, between Adams and Jefferson Streets. The meat was salted and transformed into "canned willie" (corned beef) after which it was packed in quarters at a yard on the South side of Ferry Street between First and Second Streets.

The company was successful, and the two brothers employed 100 workers and slaughtered more than 1,000 heads of cattle a week. Samuel and Ebenezer built a dock close to Ferry Street where they loaded their barrels of beef and pork into their own sloops to transport them along the Hudson River.

In 1812, war broke out again between the US and the English. Samuel and his brother contracted with Elbert Anderson, a government supplier, to provide the troops in New York and Albany with 2,000 barrels of pork and 3,000 barrels of beef.

View of a dock and sloops on the Hudson River
On the right side: one of the Robert Fulton's steamers

SAMUEL WILSON
"UNCLE SAM"

ON THURSDAY OCTOBER 1st, 1812 SAMUEL WILSON, TROY'S UNCLE SAM BECAME AMERICA'S UNCLE SAM

PREAMBLE

What it took for Samuel Wilson to become America's national symbol Uncle Sam:

* Edward Wilson gave to one of his sons the first name "Samuel".
* Samuel Wilson happened to be a talented entrepreneur and an active member of the Troy community; he was loved by the Troy population and his employees who nicknamed him "Uncle Sam".
* In 1812, the war broke again between England and the United States.
* Elbert Anderson, a government supplier, contracted with Samuel Wilson to provide the army with meat.
* The abbreviation U.S. to name the United States of America was not yet stamped in the people's mind (it was the beginning of the U.S.A.).
* The foreman of Samuel Wilson was in charge of welcoming the visitors and was adept at making jokes, and he enjoyed spreading them.
* And a curious visitor, asked a question...

LOCATION

The wharf of the E.S. Wilson Company on the Hudson River bank, at Ferry Street between First Street and Second Street in Troy, New York.

THE CAST

The visitors:
- Elbert Anderson, a government supplier
- Theodorus Bailey, Anderson's silent partner
- Governor Daniel Tompkins of New York on his way to inspect military preparations on the Niagara frontier
- His aide, Lieutenant Colonel Robert Mc Combs
- Another aide, Lieutenant John Livingstone

... and Samuel Wilson's foreman, Jonas W. Gleason, in charge of the visitors, an Irish guy nicknamed "Boss Butcher".

Continued...

SAMUEL WILSON
"UNCLE SAM"

OCTOBER 1st, 1812

ACT ONE

The five visitors arrived from Albany on the Firefly, one of Robert Fulton's steamers. They landed on the wharf of the E.S. Wilson Company where a large consignment of meat barrels for the Army was piled. They were coming to verify the delivery of meat that Elbert Anderson ordered from Samuel Wilson.

ACT TWO

One of the visitors noticed the initials E.A. U.S. on the barrels. He knew "E.A." which were the initials of Elbert Anderson, and asked Jonas Gleason who had welcomed them the significance of "U.S." written following "E.A.".

Jonas Gleason, who never missed the occasion of a joke, answered that those were Uncle Sam's initials. The passenger inquired: "Who is Uncle Sam?". Gleason's reply was: "Don't you know Uncle Sam? He owns near everything around here and he's got the best beef and he's feeding the whole army".

The answer seemed to make sense to the visitors:
E.A. = the initials of the buyer
U.S. = the initials of the seller. Why not?

UNCLE SAM WILSON OF TROY SUPPLIED BEEF TO THE UNITED STATES ARMY DURING THE WAR OF 1812~ STAMPING HIS BARRELS WITH THE LETTERS 'U.S.'~ THIS BEEF BECAME KNOWN TO THE ARMY AS "UNCLE SAM'S" AND THIS FAMILIAR APPELLATION WAS THEREAFTER BESTOWED ON OUR OWN GOVERNMENT * * *

Continued...

SAMUEL WILSON
"UNCLE SAM"

OCTOBER 1st, 1812

ACT THREE

Jonas Gleason, happy that his joke had worked, spread it everywhere in Troy, and since a lot of the soldiers were Samuel Wilson's former employees, the joke spread even faster and Uncle Sam soon became the nickname of the U.S. government.

CONCLUSION

Bailey, who witnessed the creation of the joke and later found out that it had given birth to the nickname of the U.S.A., wrote the story. His wife found his notes after his death and sent them to a newspaper, "The New York Gazette", that published it in its May 12, 1830 issue.

A transcript of this account appeared in the Book of the Navy, by John Frost, which was published in 1842.

This story was introduced by Bartlett into his Dictionary of Americanisms in 1848.

Another testimony of the story comes from the late Lucius E. Wilson of New York City. Mr. Wilson was one of Uncle Sam's great nephews.

UNCLE SAM WILSON OF TROY SUPPLIED BEEF TO THE UNITED STATES ARMY DURING THE WAR OF 1812~ STAMPING HIS BARRELS WITH THE LETTERS 'U.S.' THIS BEEF BECAME KNOWN TO THE ARMY AS 'UNCLE SAM'S' AND THIS FAMILIAR APPELLATION WAS THEREAFTER BESTOWED ON OUR OWN GOVERNMENT * * *

SAMUEL WILSON
"UNCLE SAM"

JONAS W. GLEASON

Jonas Gleason, the foreman of Samuel Wilson who was at the origin of the joke which gave Samuel the nickname of Uncle Sam, was himself nicknamed "Boss Butcher". He followed Samuel Wilson to Catskill when Samuel opened another slaughterhouse.

He was quite ambitious and loved to address the public. He always delivered a speech for the 4th of July. At the end of the meat-packing season, Jonas always led the procession of workers to the festive board, riding his horse and wearing a huge pair of bullock livers as epaulets.

He later became foreman in a ladder company and addressed the employees every month from the top of a ladder.

He finally became the town auctioneer, a job for which his voice eminently qualified him.

SAMUEL WILSON
"UNCLE SAM"

TROY
SAMUEL WILSON'S HOUSE

This is the third and last of Samuel Wilson's homes in Troy. It was located at 144 Ferry Street. He died there on July 31, 1854. Unfortunately, this house was torn down during the bicentennial.

Previously, Samuel had occupied another farmhouse at the junction of Cottage and Fifteenth Streets, at the end of Mount Ida. This area was called "Wilson's Hollow".

SAMUEL WILSON
"UNCLE SAM"

CATSKILL, NEW YORK
1817 - 1822

Samuel Wilson's father died in Troy, in 1816. Later that same year, his mother departed for Mason where she lived until the end of her life with her youngest son Thomas.

Samuel and his young brother Nathaniel moved to Catskill. There Samuel wanted to give "Nat" a start in business and create work for other men. They opened another slaughterhouse and meatpacking plant (Samuel had started his first plant with his other brother Ebenezer in Troy, in 1793). Many of Samuel's workmen from Troy moved to Catskill as well and it became a flourishing business. Samuel and Nathaniel also opened brickyards along the Catskill Creek and today the bridge spanning that creek is named the *Uncle Sam Bridge.*

Samuel and Nathaniel's families lived in a large mansion located at 251 West Main Street. That's where Martin Van Buren, the 8th President of the United States, had married Hannah Hoes in 1807, before he became president.

This historical mansion, which was built in 1797, is still standing. Two plaques in front of it remind us of the time when Samuel Wilson and Martin Van Buren were there.

Uncle Sam and Aunt Betsey were active in the First Baptist Church and town affairs in Catskill, just as they had been in Troy. However Troy was the town they had seen grow from a river hamlet to a city, and it was their true home. They returned there in 1822 to live the rest of their lives, leaving Nathaniel and his family in Catskill.

Nathaniel died in Catskill in 1854, just 19 days after his brother Samuel's death. He had four sons, one of whom became the president of the Catskill Bank.

SAMUEL WILSON
"UNCLE SAM"

TROY
OAKWOOD CEMETERY

Monument dedicated to Samuel Wilson
in 1931 by his grand-daughter,
Marion Wilson Sheldon.

Samuel descended from a long-lived family. His mother and several of his brothers were octogenarians.

After 1837, he became less active. He had been failing physically over a period of years. During the last year before his death, he remained confined to his home. He passed away there on July 31, 1854, at the age of 88.

Samuel was buried at Mount Ida cemetery and later the body was removed to Oakwood cemetery.

Betsey, who survived until 1863, was buried close to him.

Samuel and Betsey rest in the Oakwood Cemetery

SAMUEL WILSON
"UNCLE SAM"

TROY
UNCLE SAM'S MONUMENT

Monument dedicated to Samuel Wilson in 1980
Located on River Street, close to the Hudson River

*"The big thing is not what happens to us in life
but what we do about what happens to us."*
Samuel Wilson

SAMUEL WILSON
"UNCLE SAM"

SAMUEL WILSON AS "UNCLE SAM"

If he did not especially glory in his title of Uncle Sam being synonymous with United States, he nonetheless enjoyed himself a lot.

He benefited from more popularity and his social life and involvement with the community grew.

He was invited everywhere, named president at special events, officer of various clubs, addressed a lot of audiences and proposed numerous toasts!

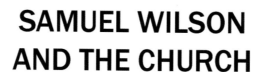

SAMUEL WILSON
"UNCLE SAM"

SAMUEL WILSON
AND THE CHURCH

The Wilson family was extremely religious. In Menotomy they attended the Congregational parish of Reverend Cook. Every evening, after the work day, Edward read and commented on a page of the Bible to his family.

When the Wilson family moved to Mason, NH, they met again with former friends and members of the Reverend Cook's parish, such as the Russells and the Winships, who preceded them to Mason. They frequented the Mason Congregational Church (Old Meeting House). Samuel became the friend of Ebenezer Hill who later became pastor in Mason. Reverend Ebenezer Hill gave Samuel and Betsey their wedding benediction in 1797.

Location of the
First Meeting House

Old Second Meeting House (Congregational) built in 1790 with the materials of the Old First Meeting House

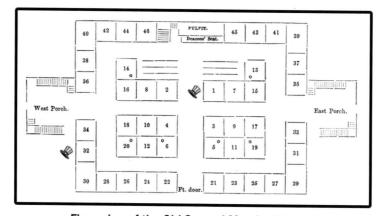

Floor plan of the Old Second Meeting House
☞ # 32: Wilson Family's pew   ☞ # 1: Mann Family's pew

SAMUEL WILSON
"UNCLE SAM"

SAMUEL WILSON
AND THE CHURCH

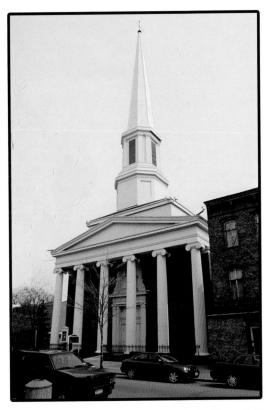

The Old Third Street Church in Troy, NY.

In Troy, Samuel was a Baptist (*Records of the Old Third Street Baptist Church testify to that fact*).

The bricks used to build the church were provided by the E. & S. Wilson company.

Samuel was elected a trustee of the church from 1808 until 1816.

He then moved to Catskill, NY, until 1822. During that period he is believed to have attended the First Baptist Church there.

SAMUEL WILSON
"UNCLE SAM"

SAMUEL WILSON
AND POLITICS

Samuel Wilson was extremely tolerant in politics, as he was in his professional and social life, as well as in religion.

Though a strong republican, he was also attached to some principles of the democratic tendency.

Invited at a democratic meeting, he proposed this toast:
"The young men of Rensselaer!
Animated by a glorious spirit of liberty, they have nobly manifested their desire of promoting the extension of republican principles."

At another meeting to honor Andrew Jackson, he offered this one:
"Hickory to lash the enemy of our country!"

Devoted to Jackson, he was offered the presidency of the committee to receive the president on his tour of New England in 1833. Wilson was twice president of the Rensselaer county committees of election and re-election of President Jackson.

In 1837 he became chairman of the democratic committee.

SAMUEL WILSON
"UNCLE SAM"

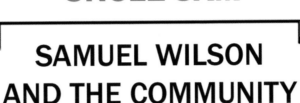

SAMUEL WILSON
AND THE COMMUNITY

From his young age Samuel Wilson was very sensitive about the community. As a schoolboy, his commitment to justice and compassion were already in evidence.

One day, during a tough winter, two young pupils were sitting in the cold back area of the classroom. Samuel asked the teacher why. The answer was that these two kids did not bring anymore wood and food to the teacher who was supported by the pupil's families. Samuel replied that these kid's parents were poor and could not actually spare any food or wood. The teacher retorted that he, too, needed food and wood to keep on teaching. Samuel asked the teacher to bring the two kids to the warmer part of the room and promised to supply their share of food and wood the following day. The teacher agreed, surprised by Samuel's request, and added: "*How is your dad, who is a* Son of Liberty, *going to react? These two kids are tories...*". Samuel said that compassion does not have political boundaries.

Samuel went back home a little worried about his promise. His family was also poor. He explained his case to his father who told him that he acted properly and that his family was going to limit themselves so that he could keep his promise.

In Mason, when he became an adult, upon Betsey's request, he delivered numerous speeches about his views of the future of his country, speeches based on equality and mutual assistance. He stunned a lot of people, separatists and federalists, who wondered how a farmer's son, who'd never lived in a large city, could generate such ideas.

SAMUEL WILSON
"UNCLE SAM"

SAMUEL WILSON
AND THE COMMUNITY

In Troy, he surprised the *patroon* of the town, Mr. Van Der Heyden, with his view of the growing settlement: "*It could be another Philadelphia with streets laid off wide and space left to grow*". He was invited to deliver speeches at the town meetings, often quoting Alexander Hamilton: "*Not only the wealth, but the independence and security of a country, appear to be materially connected with the prosperity of manufacturing... when it follows that it is in the interest of the community, with a view to eventual and permanent economy, to encourage the growth of manufacturing*".

In 1793, Troy and Lansingburgh engaged in keen competition for the honor to become the capital of Rensselaer County. The decision as to the location was to be made on the basis of which town subscribed the most to the building fund intended for a court house and a jail. Samuel pledged four pounds and his brother Ebenezer three; with a total of one thousand pounds subscribed, Troy won out the competition.

Samuel Wilson also showed humanity and benevolence. One of his speeches deeply marked the assistants of a town meeting: "*It is through real necessity that the debtors in jail make their situation known to the public. With diffidence they solicit the citizens to help them so far as to keep them from hunger; as the law gives no relief, and consequently, if unable to help themselves and unassisted by a charitable community, they must inevitably starve. One of their number is two hundred miles from his friends and family, without money for credit*".

Continued...

SAMUEL WILSON
"UNCLE SAM"

SAMUEL WILSON
AND THE COMMUNITY

Samuel and Betsey, through their kindness and the support they provided to the community earned the nick-name of Uncle Sam and Aunt Betsey of Troy.

During the 1812 war, he was the kind of man people thought of to serve on a committee to aid the families of the soldiers away in the army.

In 1816, Samuel, willing to help his younger brother Nathaniel to open his own business, and at the same time to create new jobs, moved to Catskill. He remained there until 1822. The inhabitants of Catskill, grateful for the help he brought to the town, gave the bridge spanning the river the name of Uncle Sam bridge.

Betsey Wilson was one of the six managers of the Ladies' Benevolent Society established in 1830 to render assistance to indigent women and children.

Patroon: a member of the Dutch West India Company who, on condition of planting fifty settlers within the New Netherland was granted proprietary and manorial rights to sixteen miles of frontage on the Hudson River, with all the land behind.

SAMUEL WILSON
"UNCLE SAM"

FROM SAMUEL WILSON / UNCLE SAM TO UNCLE SAM / U.S. GOVERNMENT

If Samuel Wilson was officially recognized as Uncle Sam / U. S. in 1961, unofficially Uncle Sam rapidly became the representation of the United States or the government soon after October 1, 1812.

The term "Uncle Sam" first appeared in a Troy newspaper - the Troy Post, on September 7, 1813.

The first book related to Uncle Sam as the personification of the U. S. government was published in 1816: *The Adventures of Uncle Sam, by Frederick Augustus Fidfaddy.*

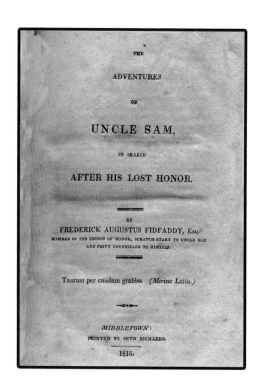

SAMUEL WILSON
"UNCLE SAM"

FROM SAMUEL WILSON / UNCLE SAM TO UNCLE SAM / U.S. GOVERNMENT

Uncle Sam really owes its national recognition to the talent of various artists:

Thomas Nast, in the 1870's, imposed the image of Uncle Sam in Harper's Weekly: long legs, tails and top hat. He had gathered information about Samuel Wilson's look from one of his relatives. He endowed him with a goatee which was in fashion at that time.

Thomas Nast created the image of Santa Claus. He also invented the symbols of the elephant for the republicans and the donkey for the democrats. He's at the origin of the word "nasty".

Thomas Nast (1840-1902)

SAMUEL WILSON
"UNCLE SAM"

FROM SAMUEL WILSON / UNCLE SAM TO UNCLE SAM / U.S. GOVERNMENT

Keppler, founder of *"Puck"*, often starred Uncle Sam on the front covers and the centerfolds of his magazines.

Joseph Keppler (1838-1894)

SAMUEL WILSON
"UNCLE SAM"

FROM SAMUEL WILSON / UNCLE SAM
TO UNCLE SAM / U.S. GOVERNMENT

Victor Gillam, like Keppler, often dedicated the front covers and centerfolds of "Judge" to Uncle Sam.

Victor Gillam (1858-1920)

SAMUEL WILSON
"UNCLE SAM"

FROM SAMUEL WILSON / UNCLE SAM
TO UNCLE SAM / U.S. GOVERNMENT

James Montgomery Flagg, in 1917, immortalized Uncle Sam's image with his poster "I Want You" which he considered himself as the "most famous poster in the world". "I Want You" is in fact a self-portrait of the artist!

James Montgomery Flagg (1877-1960)

SAMUEL WILSON
"UNCLE SAM"

FROM SAMUEL WILSON / UNCLE SAM
TO UNCLE SAM / U.S. GOVERNMENT

Charles Dana Gibson, famous for his "Gibson's Girls", gave the Uncle Sam posters a *touch of elegance* during World War One.

Charles Dana Gibson (1867-1944)

SAMUEL WILSON
"UNCLE SAM"

SAMUEL WILSON'S
FOUR TOWNS

Arlington, Massachusetts

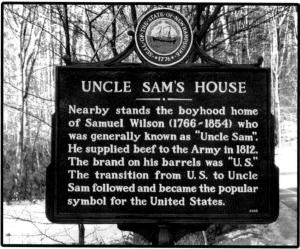

UNCLE SAM'S HOUSE

Nearby stands the boyhood home of Samuel Wilson (1766~1854) who was generally known as "Uncle Sam". He supplied beef to the Army in 1812. The brand on his barrels was "U. S." The transition from U. S. to Uncle Sam followed and became the popular symbol for the United States.

Mason, New Hampshire

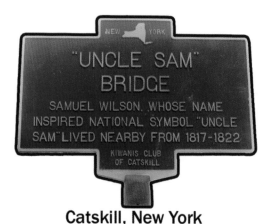

Catskill, New York

Troy, New York

WHAT HAPPENED TO
SAMUEL WILSON'S FOUR PLACES?

SAMUEL WILSON
"UNCLE SAM"

ARLINGTON, MASSACHUSETTS

It would be difficult nowadays for Samuel Wilson to recognize his birth place. The village of Menotomy, originally settled in 1635, became West Cambridge and was incorporated in 1867 and renamed Arlington to honor the heroes buried in the Arlington National Cemetery in Virginia.

Nor would he find his old farm. A monument has been erected on its former site to honor him. It's located at the intersection of the two busiest streets of Arlington (Massachusetts Avenue and Mystic Street).

At the 2000 US census, Arlington counted about 42,000 inhabitants on a land area of approximately 5.5 square miles, including 266 acres of rivers, lakes and ponds.

The Jefferson Cutter house is now the home of the Cyrus E. Dallin Art Museum and the Visitor Bureau. It's located near the Uncle Sam memorial.

SAMUEL WILSON
"UNCLE SAM"

MASON, NEW HAMPSHIRE

Should Samuel Wilson come back to Mason now, it might be the only "town" he would recognize. He could find his family farm which has been extremely well preserved by the successive owners.

Mason is certainly the most peaceful town in the United States. As per the last census, it counted about 1,100 inhabitants scattered over 24 square miles of maples and birch-trees, creeks and ponds.

Mason is the image of New Hampshire: Eighty percent forests, rivers and lakes, the state of "*live free or die*" and common sense. Mason represents the "quality of life".

The four seasons in Mason

SAMUEL WILSON
"UNCLE SAM"

MASON, NEW HAMPSHIRE

It would be unfair to mention Mason and forget Greenville (about 2,200 inhabitants at the last census / approximately 6 square miles).

At the time of the Wilson and Mann families, Greenville was part of Mason (Mason Village). The town split in 1872, and the north-west part of it was separately incorporated under the name of Greenville.

The town is located on the upper falls of the Souhegan River whose plentiful water power provided the town with the first state industries: making cotton and wool goods.

Greenville waterfalls, historical mills and buildings
and the Uncle Sam Inn and Museum
(former Columbia Manufacturing Boarding house)

SAMUEL WILSON
"UNCLE SAM"

TROY, NEW YORK

If Troy played an important role in the life of Samuel Wilson, it can be said that Samuel Wilson also played an important role in the expansion of Troy. He belonged to the first generation which started developing the town.

When he arrived in 1789, there were fewer than four hundred inhabitants. In 1816, when Troy was recorded as a city, it counted almost 4,500 people. At the last 2004 census, the population was around 48,000 with a land area of approximately 10.4 square miles.

The first quarter of the nineteenth century saw Troy expand and become a leading town in various specialties. It's been considered as the birth place of the "industrial revolution".

Troy, the "collar city": Hannah Lord Montagne created the first detachable collar. At the beginning of the nineteenth century, fifteen thousand people worked in the collar industry and ninety percent of the collars worn in the USA were produced in Troy. Wearing a detachable white collar gave rise to a new working social class - the "white collar" employee, distinct from the factory "blue collar" worker.

In 1875, twenty-three companies produced more than four million dollars in ovens and employed two thousand workers.

In 1881, the Burden Iron Company produced almost all the horse-shoes necessary to the Northern Army during the Civil War (fifty one million horse-shoes a year!).

Troy, New York. 2005.

SAMUEL WILSON
"UNCLE SAM"

TROY, NEW YORK

Troy, "capital of the bells": The foundries of Troy provided about one hundred thousand bells to the USA. The bells were famous for the quality of their sound and workmanship. A foundry from Troy, the Meneely Foundry, cast the bell to replace the *Liberty Bell* for the celebration of the centennial in 1876.

Troy became an important center of science in the USA, with the opening of the famous school "Rensselaer Polytechnic Institute" which was the first college of sciences in the USA,

Emma Willard started the first American women's college, the *Emma Willard School,* in Troy in 1821. It later became the *Russell Sage College for Women.*

Troy, New York. 2005.

SAMUEL WILSON
"UNCLE SAM"

TROY, NEW YORK

TROY's FAMOUS PEOPLE:

- Amos Eaton, known as the "father of American geology" was the founder of the Rensselaer Polytechnic Institute,

- Joseph Henry, a student of Eaton, became the first director of the Smithsonian Institute.

- James Hall, another student of Amos Eaton, was known as the "father of the geosyncline". He's also considered to be the father of American paleontology.

- In sports, four great boxers come from Troy:
  - John Morrissey who won the heavyweight championship of America in 1853
  - Puddy Ryan who won the first true world heavyweight championship in 1880
  - John C. Heenan aka the "Benicia Boy" who, in 1860, fought in England the most incredible combat: 41 rounds, over two hours,
  - and... Mike Tyson who started his career under the leadership of Troy's Uncle Sam Boxing Club. His first fight occured in Troy in 1986.

We recommend "Troy, A Collar City History" by Don Rittner.

Monument erected in 1890 to honor Rensselaer County soldiers and sailors who served in the Civil War.

SAMUEL WILSON
"UNCLE SAM"

TROY
PRESENCE OF UNCLE SAM

SAMUEL WILSON
"UNCLE SAM"

CATSKILL, NEW YORK

Catskill, NY, Circa 1910

Though Samuel Wilson stayed in Catskill for only six years, he successfully launched two companies which created numerous new jobs. He was much appreciated by the Catskill residents.

Samuel's brother, Nathaniel, remained a Catskill resident until his death in 1854.

At the last census, the population of Catskill was about 12,000. Catskill land area is approximately 2.2 square miles.

SAMUEL WILSON
"UNCLE SAM"

CATSKILL, NEW YORK

"UNCLE SAM"
SAMUEL WILSON, "UNCLE SAM"
THE OFFICIAL SYMBOL OF
THE UNITED STATES
LIVED HERE 1817 TO 1823

MARTIN
VAN BUREN
8TH PRESIDENT OF THE U.S.
WAS MARRIED IN THIS HOUSE
TO HANNAH HOES IN 1807.
HOUSE BUILT IN 1797.
STATE EDUCATION
DEPARTMENT 1932

"UNCLE SAM"
BRIDGE
SAMUEL WILSON, WHOSE NAME
INSPIRED NATIONAL SYMBOL "UNCLE
SAM" LIVED NEARBY FROM 1817-1822
KIWANIS CLUB
OF CATSKILL

Two signs remind us of the
presence of Samuel Wilson
in Catskill: One in front of the
mansion where he lived and
the other one on the bridge.

SAMUEL WILSON
"UNCLE SAM"

CONCLUSION

Dear Reader:

We hope that through this book you discovered the life of our national symbol and also the little stories that make the history.

To better appreciate what this first American generation accomplished, one has to recall the conditions of this era: no electricity, no cars, no computers, phones, etc... only strong legs and arms, and an unsinkable will to build their new country.

Nowadays, it takes an hour and a half by car from Arlington, MA, to Mason, NH, on a smooth paved road. Imagine a pair of oxen pulling a wagon stuffed with the family's possessions, and nine children, through dirt roads roughly drawn.

Imagine the two Wilson brothers walking from Mason, NH, to Troy, NY, during a cold winter, through New Hampshire, Vermont and part of New York, for fifteen days, with no money.

Imagine the eighty-year old Samuel Whittemore, shot, bayoneted, beaten and left for dead who survived without antibiotics or anesthesia to live until 98 years of age.

Imagine Paul Revere riding from Boston to New York or Philadelphia to deliver his messages.

These are but a few examples...

We can be proud of our ancestors. Let's honor them.

SAMUEL WILSON
"UNCLE SAM"

WE'D LIKE TO THANK ALL THE PEOPLE WHO HELPED US AND SUPPORTED US IN OUR PROJECTS, ESPECIALLY:

Mr. Murray Segal
Mrs. Kathleen Baglio Humphreys
Mr. Howard Winkler, Mrs. Doreen Stevens, Mr. Paul Hogman,
Mr. John Gearin, and the Arlington Historical Society
Mrs. Peg Schuster, Mrs. and Mr. Ginie and Arthur Rafter,
Mrs. Barbara Schulze and the Mason Historical Society
Mrs. Susan Wolpert and Mrs. Denise Ginzler and the Mason Public Library
Mrs. Barbara Milkovits
Mrs. and Mr. Tina and Mike McGuire
Mrs. and Mr. Penny and John Savard
Mr. Richard Eaton
Mrs. and Mr. Gil Bliss
Mr. Eric Moskowitz
Mr. William Copeley and the New Hampshire Historical Society
Mrs. Virginia Drew, Mr. Ken Leidner and the NH State House Visitor Center
Tom and Ray Clement
Mr. Sandy Horowitz
Mr. George Jacques
Mr. Frederick Polnisch
Mrs. and Mr. Kristina and Deric Torres
Mr. David Wishingrad
Mr. Preston Cook
Dr. Ellen Wagner and Ms. Anne Derryberry
Ms. Pat Veitch
Mrs. Mary Anne Stapleton
Mr. Dan McInnis
Mr. Basile Fattal

SAMUEL WILSON
"UNCLE SAM"

WHAT THEY THINK ABOUT OUR BOOK

"Excellent presentation and very informative. The photos in the book uniquely joins Sam Wilson's life and family with America's independence and how he became our national symbol of Uncle Sam. The book presents the humanity of Uncle Sam."

Fred Polnisch - Clifton Park, NY
Performer and author of "Uncle Sam, My Story"

Praise to Jean-Pierre and Cecile!
Truly a magnificent book about our national symbol, and our rich, colorful history. A book that should be in every American home and all schools.

Kristina and Deric Torres - Sonoma, Ca

Bravo! You succeeded in writing a book for all, children and adults. We are not assiduous readers however, as soon as we opened the first page,we wanted to know more and read it completely. Now we know "Uncle Sam" and through him historical facts of the American Revolution that you perfectly illustrated.
A perfect scheme for a movie or a TV series.

A+++++++

Elie Maghames - San Francisco, Ca

Each time I read your book "Who Was Uncle Sam" I realize how much work, effort, design and writing skills went into it, making it so good. I use it as a reference book now.

George W. Jacques - Troy, NY
Founder of the Uncle Sam Memorial Foundation
and Author of "The Life and Times of Uncle Sam"